FRESH BREAD
DEVOTIONAL

BY DR. DAN BOLIN

aBM

Published by:

A Book's Mind

PO Box 272847

Fort Collins, CO 80527

www.abooksmind.com

Copyright © 2016

ISBN: 978-1-944255-03-9

Printed in the United States of America

DEDICATION

This book is dedicated to the hundreds of thousands of faithful volunteers around the world who serve God's Kingdom through the ministry of Christian camping. Thank you for being the hands and feet of Jesus on earth. You make a daily impact for eternity.

TABLE OF CONTENTS

PREFACE

Fresh Bread is a weekly devotional sent to Christian camping leaders and those who support their work. The *Fresh Bread* devotions are part of the more comprehensive package that includes prayer requests, calendar updates, and other information to benefit the international community of Christian camping.

Fresh Bread devotions attempt to apply the timeless truth of God's Word to a moment in real life. Writing these has helped me find application for God's truth in every moment and every area of my life. It is a healthy discipline to look for God's hand in every circumstance.

REFRESH, the 2016 CCI-Worldwide Summit at HeronBridge near Johannesburg, South Africa, motivated us to pull together thirty-one of these devotions and package them in a book to say *THANK YOU* to those who engage in any way in Christian camping around the world. As the name implies, the goal of the conference is to *Refresh* those who attend. We hope to refresh each participant with spiritual and personal encouragement, to refresh them professionally with the most current information possible, and to refresh the memories of what

God has done through Christian camping for genera-
tions. Fresh Bread is a part of this refreshing process.

The staff members at CCI-Worldwide are always
helpful to bring potential *Fresh Bread* ideas to my attention. Once I write them, Leslie Strader uses her talents
to make them better. Leslie has been instrumental in
moving this project from "one more of Dan's ideas" to
reality. Marty Putman added her thoughtful insights and
expert proofreading eye. Gwen Bowen and Hannah
Bolin made their significant contributions as well.

I also want to thank Floyd Orfield at A Book's Mind
Publishing. He and his staff have provided a steady hand
as this project moved through each stage of development.

INTRODUCTION

Throughout the Bible, bread is a symbol for life-giving sustenance. The Israelites carried bread without leaven on their exodus from Egypt (Exodus 12:34). Every Sabbath, twelve loaves were placed on a gold table in the tabernacle (Leviticus 24:5-9). David's men received 200 loaves of bread from Ziba as they escaped from Absalom (2 Samuel 16:1). Elijah helped sustain the Sidonian widow and her son with the ingredients for bread (1 Kings 17:7-16). Jesus took five loaves and two fish and fed 5,000 people. He also said:

> *I am the bread of life. He who comes to me will never go hungry* (John 6:35).

And He broke bread at the last supper telling his disciples:

> *This is my body given for you; do this in remembrance of me* (Luke 22:19).

Bread is bread, but it takes many forms around the world. The soft flat breads of East Africa are very unlike the heavy dark breads of Northern Europe. A South

American tortilla is very different from a North American sourdough loaf. Even within one country there are many varieties of bread. Here in the USA, we have biscuits, croissants, dinner rolls, hamburger buns, whole wheat, pumpernickel, blueberry muffins, bagels ... and on and on. They are all unique varieties of bread. There are also bread cousins: pancakes, cupcakes, waffles, angel food cake, devil's food cake, and cookies. Whatever the variety, bread is the foundation of God's basic provision to sustain our lives.

For all the styles of bread, Jesus makes it clear that we need more than physical food to sustain our souls. In Matthew 4:4 Jesus reviews a statement from Deuteronomy 8:3 and says, *"Man does not live by bread alone but by every word from the mouth of God."* The bread of this world is fine and necessary, but the Word of God is critical for our spiritual health and strength. Our souls need fresh bread from the mouth of God the way our bodies need a slice of toast in the morning, a hamburger bun at noon, or a dinner roll in the evening.

Bread tastes best when it is fresh out of the oven. In Matthew 6:11 Jesus prayed a remarkable prayer. He asked his Father, *"give us this day our daily bread."* Not yesterday's stale information, but something fresh for today. One or two big servings on Sunday is wonderful. We need the feasts that our pastors serve each week.

We need full meals provided by Bible study teachers, snacks from Christian radio, and refreshment from Christian writers. But ultimately, we need to feed ourselves.

This little book, *Fresh Bread*, provides thirty-one snacks to tide you over between meals, connecting short insights from God's Word to daily life. It is written with Christian camp staff members in mind—whose busy lives of service may seduce them into thinking that life is mainly about doing for God rather than connecting deeply with Him. A slice of *Fresh Bread* is good for everyone; the truth of God's Word applies to all of us and benefits us in every situation.

These spiritual snacks are short, just a few hundred words each. Sit back, nibble on a piece of *Fresh Bread*, and enjoy the spiritual health and strength they provide.

THE MISSION, VISION, AND VALUES OF CHRISTIAN CAMPING INTERNATIONAL

MISSION

The mission of Christian Camping International-Worldwide is to promote Christian camping throughout the world as a means of helping the Church fulfill the Great Commission of Jesus Christ.

VISION

The vision of Christian Camping International-Worldwide is for Christian camping to be a highly effective and highly valued ministry tool throughout the world supported by a growing alliance of internally strong, sustainable, and growth-focused associations of Christian camps and camping leaders.

VALUES

The shared values of Christian Camping International-Worldwide are:

UNITY

We value the global bonding found in a common faith, a singular purpose and shared values.

AUTONOMY

We value the variety of unique methods of organization, operation, training, networking, and promotion found throughout the world.

SHARING

We value the sharing of successful practices, resources, and prayer support.

COMMUNITY

We value the powerful and positive life transformation that occurs in relational ministry.

GROWTH

We value the wise use of resources, improving performance, and the expanding influence of Christian Camping.

SUSTAINABILITY

We value principles and practices that assure good financial stewardship, responsible management, and long-term results.

For more information about Christian Camping International-Worldwide, visit www.cciworldwide.org

CHRISTIAN CAMPING INTERNATIONAL: FACTS AND FIGURES

Christian Camping International (CCI) is an alliance of twenty-one autonomous Christian camping associations that collectively serve about 10,500,000 campers and guests annually. The camps, conferences, retreats, and outdoor ministries that comprise these associations utilize over 200,000 volunteers and host hundreds of training events each year.

Most CCI associations serve one country; however, five of the members are regional associations serving multiple countries in their parts of the world. Together, CCI associations support the work of Christian camping in sixty-one countries.

Use the code below to find the most current information about Christian camping and locate Christian camps, conference centers, retreats, and outdoor ministries in your area.

DAY 1
THE BURLS OF LIFE

While in the Ukraine, I spent some solitary time in a thick, evergreen forest reflecting on God's goodness and the glory revealed in His creation.

Sitting on a mossy log, I observed numerous trees with large burls about ten to fifteen feet (three to five meters) off the ground. Above the enlarged and disfigured section, the trees grew straight and tall.

In researching burls, I discovered that they result from an injury, fungus, or virus. The damaged and distorted portion of the tree is not pretty. But the wood of a burl is highly prized and of great value because of the beautiful swirls in its grain. In the hands of a master craftsman, wood that has been damaged and marred finds beauty and value it could not have known apart from the pain.

We all face times of heartache and injury. None of us escape the burls of life for long. But God is in the business of making all things new. Psalm 23 has four marvelous words that capture God's heart for His injured and suffering people:

He restores my soul (Psalm 23:3).

Don't waste your pain. Give it to God and allow him to restore your soul with greater beauty and increased value.

DAY 2
THE DISCIPLE JESUS LOVED

Throughout his Gospel, John refers to himself as *the disciple whom Jesus loved*. John's identity was built upon his awareness of God's love for him. He knew he was loved, and that reality shaped John's view of himself and his world.

Our lives are not designed to be empty; they long to be full. And they will be filled with something. John knew the joy and fulfillment of a life saturated with the love of Jesus.

When we lack satisfaction and peace, our focus is likely on the wrong things. Money, pleasure, drugs, busyness, popularity, recognition, accomplishment, power, control, isolation, music, alcohol, cars, clothes, artistry, sports, even church, camp, and ministry can become artificial replacements for the love we all desire.

John is the only Gospel writer to record Jesus' words, "*I have come that they may have life, and have it to the full*" (John 10:10). He knew Jesus' love, and it filled his life.

John's Gospel showed God's love for the world. His three short epistles show how love overflowed to others. But before love changed John's relationships, it changed his heart. First and foremost, he was *the disciple Jesus loved.*

What would be different if the primary perception of myself was, "*I am the disciple that Jesus loves?*" How would I treat others? How would I spend my time and money? And how would I feel about the unworthy things that compete for my affections?

DAY 3
METEOR SPRINKLE

I got up at three o'clock in the morning to see a meteor shower. I'm not sure what I expected, but certainly more than what I saw. I stood in the field by my house looking into the northeastern summer sky with my head tilted backward until I was dizzy. In ten to fifteen minutes, I saw two wimpy shooting stars. I tried to convince myself that I saw two others, but they might have been fireflies. I went back to bed.

Life is full of disappointments: the promotion goes to someone else, the doctor's report is not good, flat tires, lost keys, computer errors, spilled milk, a meteor "sprinkle" instead of a shower, and the list goes on and on.

Psalm 18:30a says, "*As for God, his way is perfect.*" That is very comforting to me. In the midst of events that unfold in unexpected, and—at times, disappointing ways—we can trust God whose way is perfect. When we spend too much time wallowing in the mire of *what if*, *I wish*, or *if only*, we lose sight of God's perfect way.

So, when a friend lets you down – *as for God, his way is perfect*. When your child's life goes off track – *as for*

God, his way is perfect. When finances are tight. . . for the third month in a row – *as for God, his way is perfect.* We must take a step back and trust the One who not only sees the road ahead, but will lead us all the way.

Don't allow disappointment to rob you of the joy of trusting God with things that are beyond your control. Trust God until the shooting star of His glory streaks across the sky of your life, reminding you that *His way is perfect.*

DAY 4
TO THE RESCUE

Gilligan's Island is a television program that ran in the United States from 1964 until 1967 and remains a popular throwback comedy on cable TV and other outlets.

A three-hour cruise goes terribly wrong and seven people find themselves stranded on a deserted island. Every attempt to escape the island meets with failure. Each episode brought new hope, but ultimately ended in futility.

The people on the island were lost and wanted to go home. And each had a gift that in other situations would have been helpful and beneficial. However, on the island these gifts were useless.

- The Captain's power could not get them off the island
- The Millionaire's wealth was of no benefit getting off the island
- Ginger and MaryAnn's beauty was not helpful getting off the island
- The Professor's education and intelligence were of no help finding a way off the island

- Gilligan's nice and helpful spirit could not get them off the island

We are all lost and isolated from God. And we cannot get off the island unless a savior comes to rescue us. Fortunately, God sent us a Savior. Paul reminds the Romans and us of this great truth: *"but God shows his love for us in that while we were still sinners, Christ died for us"* (Romans 5:8).

DAY 5
SWEET SOUNDS OF STRESS

Stringed instruments fascinate me. The music of a piano, harp, or guitar is beautiful only when the strings are under stress. If a string is too tight, it produces a sound that is sharp—but without enough tension, the sound is flat. But "just right" is truly music to my ears!

Stress is not a good thing or a bad thing; it is just a part of life. Both too much or too little tension can be problematic. Those who study such things call good stress *eustress*. Eustress spurs us on to do more and perform at higher levels. The right amount of pressure inspires us to be alert and ready for new and exciting challenges.

Paul explains the value of tension to Timothy when he says, *"If anyone sets his heart on being an overseer, he desires a noble task"* (1 Timothy 3:1).

The Greek word translated "*sets his heart*" has at its root the idea of *stretching*. Paul challenges Timothy to stretch himself and to develop leaders who are willing to take on the tension of overseeing God's church.

Don't live a flat life by avoiding the challenge of greater leadership opportunities. But don't wind yourself so tight that you sound sharp and unpleasant to those around you. Only with the right amount of tension will your life be in tune with what God intends.

DAY 6
THE LOVE OF A FATHER

Just before our nine year-old-daughter, Catie, died of leukemia on October 31, 1990, I was driving a back road in East Texas and arguing with God. At one point, I made the statement, "You have no idea what I'm going through."

Then a clear—but inaudible—voice came back, "Oh, yes I do." The impression continued, "You are fighting to save your daughter. I could have saved my Son. But I loved you enough to let Him die—so that I could save you."

God rarely communicates with me in such a personal way. Time stood still.

Emotions I didn't know I had welled up. I found myself weeping on the side of the road. And I've never since doubted God's love for me. Lots of other struggles, sins, and questions come and go, but God's love for me was answered on that lonely country road.

We tend to focus on Jesus loving us enough to die for us—which is powerful indeed. But love that allows a parent to watch His one and only Son die—when He had the power to intervene—is truly astounding.

The first Bible verse many of us learn takes on deep meaning when we reflect on the Father's pain that made this possible:

For God so loved the world that he gave his one and only Son, that whoever believes in him shall not perish but have eternal life
(John 3:16).

DAY 7
LET YOUR LOVE GROW

I've never taken a class in physics, but people who understand such things tell me that energy cannot be created. All that there is, is all that there is.

Fortunately, such restrictions are limited to the physical world; the spiritual domain is much more dynamic and free from the constraints of time and space.

Love is one of those dynamic elements that knows no limits. Paul reminded the Thessalonians, *"May the Lord make your love increase and overflow for each other and for everyone else, just as ours does for you"* (1 Thessalonians 3:12).

Increasing love is a goal we should all pursue. But we should be aware that the opportunity for growth and expansion carries with it the threat of regression. Jesus warned his disciples, *"Because of the increase of wickedness, the love of most will grow cold"* (Matthew 24:12).

Avoid the selfishness, pride, and wickedness that inhibit love or diminish its growth. Do, think, say, and believe the things that grow your love for God and others.

DAY 8
TEAM COLORS

When I attend a Texas Rangers baseball game, I rummage through my closet until I find my beloved Texas Rangers jersey. I can't watch a live Rangers game without it!

Millions and millions of dollars are spent each year on sports clothing. Hats, jackets, jerseys, and sweaters all show support for one's favorite team. Fans love to identify with their home team and much-loved players.

Putting on the jersey announces to the world our allegiance to a team. Wearing their emblem demonstrates our loyalty. Wearing a team's jersey also means that our behavior will reflect on the team we represent.

Our conduct should be consistent with our commitments. Our actions should demonstrate the true devotion of our hearts. When we put on the colors of one team, it means we will quit rooting for their opponents. Paul said:

> *Put on the new self, created to be like God in true righteousness and holiness. Therefore each of you must put off falsehood and speak*

truthfully to his neighbor, for we are all members of one body (Ephesians 4:24-25).

Put on our new self, created to be like Christ, and live life in a way that demonstrates loyalty to the team you represent.

Day 9
Stay, Seek, and Share

Asaph struggled with the inequities of life. His faith was shaken, and he was driven to the brink of despair when he compared his struggles to the comfort, prosperity, and health of his wicked counterparts.

Asaph began Psalms 73:

> *My feet had almost slipped; I had nearly lost*
> *my foothold, for I envied the arrogant when I*
> *saw the prosperity of the wicked. They have no*
> *struggles; their bodies are healthy and strong*
> (Psalm 73:2-4).

Life is filled with inequities and complex questions. Asaph was honest enough to identify his feelings and express his struggle. But he wisely clung to God in the midst of his questions. Reflecting deeply on his perplexing circumstance led him not to despair and frustration, but to learning and growth.

Asaph's final verse says:

But as for me, it is good to be near God. I have made the Sovereign Lord my refuge; I will tell of all your deeds (Psalm 73:28).

After grappling with God in this difficult Psalm, three fundamental commitments emerge. Asaph determined to stay close to God, seek protection in God alone, and share with others what God was doing in his life.

And so should we.

DAY 10
HEAVENLY HANDIWORK

For many years, I helped my wife at church with the pre-school children—little ones as young as two years old, to the big, grown-up, five-year-old boys and girls.

Every week, they made a craft project to take home and grace their refrigerator door—colored crayon rainbows scribbled above, inside, and beneath Noah's Ark; cut-out paper disciples missing legs or head; cotton-ball sheep glued to a picture of David the shepherd boy.

The parents clapped with delight, swooned with amazement, and gushed praise upon the young artists. The projects were the work of the children's little hands. These artistic creations demonstrated the children's skills, limited as they were.

Reflecting on God's handiwork, David says, "*The skies proclaim the work of his hands*" (Psalm 19:1b). The beauty of a blue sky, the delicacy of a puffy cloud, the warmth of the sun, the mystery of the moon, the wonder of the stars are all the work of God's hands. The detail is exquisite, the expanse is immeasurable, the majesty is, well, indescribable.

Take time to enjoy the beauty of God's heavenly handiwork. What we enjoy is what God made in arts and crafts—the work of His hands. Take a good look at His creative wonder and remember, God created it for our enjoyment and His glory. Then imagine what he has in store for you.

DAY 11
SPIRITUAL PASSPORT

Traveling internationally often involves two significant documents—a passport and a visa. The passport identifies my citizenship and reminds me where home is. The visa indicates the country I have permission to visit.

When traveling the world, it is difficult to mistake my passport for a visa. But when it comes to the spiritual world, I tend to get my passport and my visa turned around.

Too often I think that I'm a citizen of earth with a visa that will give me access to heaven someday. In reality, my spiritual passport identifies my citizenship in the Kingdom of God while my visa gives me permission to visit this world.

Being born with dual Jewish and Roman citizenship, Paul understood the complications and significance of these issues. He reminded the Greek/Macedonian Christians of Philippi about their identity when he said, *"But our citizenship is in heaven"* (Philippians 3:20a).

Earthly citizenship is valuable and significant. However, as Christians, we must never confuse our identity as citizens of heaven with the temporary visa privileges of earth.

DAY 12
THE SOLE OF OUR SOULS

My normally tranquil morning jog was aggravated by an annoying pebble that found its way into the bottom of my right shoe. The small stone was tolerable, but it was still a bother. Eventually, I manipulated it to a safe spot in an opening next to my big toe. Just as I became comfortable and regained my stride, it moved. The distraction, pain, annoyance, and possible injury returned.

The only real solution was to stop, remove the stone, and then resume my run.

Life puts stones in our shoes. A stone of selfish ambition, pride, greed, lust, anger, or envy can turn up in the sole of our soul. At first it is a distraction, but then we find a way to tolerate the pebble, knowing full well it doesn't belong.

Eventually, we need to deal with the issue and remove the stone that is distracting our attention. If left unchecked, it can do serious damage.

The apostle John understood the pebbles of pride, fear, and anger. He wrote:

> *My dear children, I write this to you so that*
> *you will not sin. But if anybody does sin, we*

*have one who speaks to the Father in our
defense—Jesus Christ, the Righteous One. He
is the atoning sacrifice for our sins, and not only
for ours but also for the sins of the whole world*
(1 John 2:1-2).

If you have a pebble in your shoe, stop and remove it. Maybe it is a new problem or maybe you have lived with it a long time. Don't allow it to distract your attention or damage your future. Jesus came to take the stones away so that we can walk with Him step-by-step, free from distraction and danger.

Day 13
Eating an Elephant

An African friend posed the age-old question, "How do you eat an elephant?"

I responded knowingly, "One bite at a time!"

He smiled and said, "No. In Africa, we invite the whole family!"

What a great answer! From my cultural and personal background, I had to eat it all by myself. I must own my problems and face life's daunting challenges alone. My prideful, default approach is to do it all myself.

From my African friend's perspective, admitting that he was outmatched by the task and calling for reinforcements was the only logical solution. Humility allowed him to ask for help, benefiting himself and supplying the needs of the people around him. Asking for assistance is a win-win proposition.

Paul reminds us that we should not face life's challenges alone; we need each other. *"Carry each other's burdens, and in this way you will fulfill the law of Christ."* But the next verse explains the deeper reason why: *"If anyone thinks he is something when he is nothing, he deceives himself"* (Galatians 6:2-3).

We cannot eat the elephant, even if we try. One bite at a time will never work. If we think we can do it alone, we deceive ourselves. Big challenges require help and asking for help requires humility. Don't chew on your own problems. Set the table, and invite family and friends to help.

DAY 14
THE RAIN IN SPAIN

I carried my raincoat all over Europe. In Spain, the forecast predicted rain every third day, so I thought I'd made a good decision by bringing it along. Most days were magnificent: cool, sunny, brisk—a few clouds, but no rain.

A few drops greeted us as we began a tour of Segovia, but the sky was mostly clear. Drops turned to drizzle and by the time we reached the farthest corner of the city square, the sky turned dark and the rain started in earnest. Unfortunately, my "good decision" was still packed in my suitcase back in my room.

Raincoats only work when we put them on. And there are a host of spiritual qualities that will benefit us and others only when we *"put them on."* In Colossians 3:12-14, Paul tells us to, *"clothe yourselves with compassion, kindness, humility, gentleness and patience. And over all these virtues put on love, which binds them all together in perfect unity."*

Way too often, I leave my kindness, humility, gentleness, patience, and love in the suitcase back in my room. I need to put them on for them to benefit me and those I meet.

The more you wear these Christ-like qualities, the more comfortable they feel. Start a fashion statement in your home, office, church, school, or neighborhood by wearing the spiritual qualities that make you look good, and inspire others to wear them as well.

Day 15
Rich in Faith

I recently saw a list of the 100 richest people in the world, those who had accumulated enough cash to buy a small nation. But are they really rich? Does a person's financial net worth truly reflect how wealthy they are?

We measure worth in dollars, pounds, rubles, yen, or some other form of currency. But God has a different standard. James reminds us, "*Has not God chosen those who are poor in the eyes of the world to be rich in faith and to inherit the kingdom he promised those who love him*?" (James 2:5).

Faith and love seem to be of greater value than the ability to accumulate silver and gold. The faith that allows us to relate to God, and the love that responds to Him and the people around us, are of significant value. And our relationships of faith and love will last forever!

I imagine that God has a list as well. But at the top of His will be a group of people who are known to only a handful of close friends, yet have accumulated treasure chests of faith and love.

DAY 16
A SCRATCH IN THE VINYL

A friend showed me his collection of 1960s and 1970s vinyl records. Not only did he have the albums, he had a turntable with a needle!

When we turned on the record player, the music and memories flowed. Remembering the good times associated with the songs was delightful—for a while. Our joy was soon interrupted by the all-too-familiar scratch and replay of the same line in the same song over and over. A scratch in the vinyl blocked the song from moving forward, and time and time again, we heard repeated lyrics and tunes.

Sometimes, we get stuck. Sometimes, we come to the same testing and use the same excuses, experiencing the same failed results.

Paul's life was filled with scratches and repeated challenges. He said, "*Do not conform any longer to the pattern of this world, but be transformed by the renewing of your mind. Then you will be able to test and approve what God's will is—his good, pleasing and perfect will*" (Romans 12:2).

A very loose paraphrase might read: *don't let the scratches of life stop you from singing the song God has composed for you. Get past the issues that are interrupting the music by transforming your mind. Then your life will be part of God's grand musical.*

DAY 17
A LION OF SIGHT

The hiking trail was clearly marked with signs announcing that bear and mountain lions roamed the area. But none of the six adults and seven children really took the warning seriously until a mountain lion walked out of the brush and crossed our path.

Fortunately, he was not hungry, and kept on walking. We hurried back to the cars, proud to have seen this amazing animal—and lived to tell about it. We continued our hike with a greater sense of caution and awareness of the possible dangers surrounding us.

As Peter brings his first letter to a close, he writes, *"Be self-controlled and alert. Your enemy the devil prowls around like a roaring lion looking for someone to devour. Resist him, standing firm in the faith"* (1 Peter 5:8-9a).

When it comes to spiritual things, we face an even greater danger. The warnings are there; the threat is real, and we need to be alert. Temptation comes in many forms and they can all be deadly. Greed, lust, anger, pride, and selfishness can all destroy our effectiveness in ministry.

Watch out for the spiritual mountain lions that stalk your life. Be aware of the threats. And walk close to the One who provides your ultimate protection.

DAY 18
POWER SOURCE

If I were emperor of the world, I would make a few changes. Things would be a little less complicated as I travel the globe. We would all drive on the same side of the road, measure temperature with the same scale, write on a common-sized paper, and most of all, have one style of electrical plugs.

Very few things are more frustrating than the inability to recharge a dead computer or cell phone due to the lack of an electrical adapter. Power is within the wall, but inaccessible.

One critical component is missing: the connecter between the source of power and the dead battery. Without that essential link, the power will never flow into the lifeless battery. The connector is critical.

Paul reminded Timothy of the critical connection between his needy life and the source of all power. He wrote, "*For there is one God and one mediator between God and men, the man Christ Jesus*" (1 Timothy 2:5).

The one and only Connector between the dead battery of our spiritual lives and the all-sufficient power of God is Jesus Christ. And He works in every culture, language, and location on the earth.

DAY 19
OPOSSUM RELOCATION

My wife opened the door to our garage and discovered an opossum helping himself to dinner at our cat's meal dish. I was called to catch the critter, but before I could get there, he disappeared behind an array of tools, boxes, and Christmas decorations. I couldn't catch him; I couldn't find him. He seemed to have disappeared.

A few days later, I opened the outside doors to the garage and pulled boxes and tools away from the wall. Then I started the leaf blower. Eventually, the opossum scampered out from behind a rack of tools and cowered in the corner. Pointing the full force of the blower at him, the creature finally surrendered and ran for his life down the driveway, through the woods, and across the street.

Even though the opossum was not designed to live in a garage, he had moved in and become comfortable. The opossum had no motivation to leave and live life the way he was designed—until he faced the leaf blower.

Powerful emotional "leaf blowers" such as fear, sorrow, or pain may be the tools God uses to get our attention and move us out of an inappropriate area of comfort and in the direction He has designed for us to go.

Paul understood God's use of the painful Damascus Road experience to redirect his life, and he applied the same strategy to the Corinthians. He wrote:

> *Even if I caused you sorrow by my letter, I do not regret it. Though I did regret it—I see that my letter hurt you, but only for a little while—yet now I am happy, not because you were made sorry, but because your sorrow led you to repentance* (2 Corinthians 7:8-9a).

Don't wait for the leaf blower or pain to redirect your life. Take stock of your behaviors, thoughts, and attitudes, and be quick to move out of areas that provide comfort, but do not help you become the person you were designed to be.

DAY 20
HAVE FUN

I visited a camp once that had a sign listing several rules to be observed while at the pool. They included the standard: NO RUNNING, NO DIVING IN THE SHALLOW END and several other common-sense prohibitions. The last rule was the one that caught my eye: HAVE FUN! The warnings were coupled with a reward. If we follow the rules, we reap the benefit of an enjoyable experience.

Psalm 19 emphasizes the value and impact of Scripture. After listing a series of descriptions and benefits of God's Word in verses 7-9, David says, *"By them is your servant warned; in keeping them there is great reward"* (Psalm 19:11).

Like the sign at the pool, God's Word contains directives that warn us away from danger and help us enjoy life to the fullest. When we disregard God's warnings and act independently, we flirt with danger. When we follow the rules and live within the guidelines of Scripture, we enjoy a rewarding life.

DAY 21
THE AERODYNAMICS OF HOPE

When I'm at 35,000 feet above the Atlantic, I try not to think about how much the airplane weighs. I'm always amazed that the vacuum created by the curve of a rapidly-moving wing can lift tons of airplane, baggage, passengers and me off the ground. As much as gravity is pulling us down, aerodynamics is lifting us up.

Forces are always at work to lift us up and pull us down. Isaiah reminds us, *"Even youths grow tired and weary, and young men stumble and fall; but those who hope in the Lord will renew their strength. They will soar on wings like eagles; they will run and not grow weary, they will walk and not be faint"* (Isaiah 40:30-31).

Despair, discouragement, and disappointment are forces that can weigh heavily upon us—they would love to pull us down. Hope lifts us up. But hope is not enough; what we place hope *in* is critical. We can hope in our skills, strength, money, friends, or education. But Isaiah reminds us that our hope must be in the Lord.

Soar above the adversity today by placing your hope in the Lord. His power to lift you up is stronger than the forces at work to pull you down.

DAY 22
SATURATION AND RUNOFF

The rain started as a drizzle, refreshing the parched Texas ground. The longer and harder it rained, the more the earth absorbed the water and eventually, became saturated.

Usually, we don't complain about rain here in Texas, but day after day, the heavens opened and soaked the ground, turning everything into a soggy mess. Mud puddles turned into small ponds; drainage ditches filled to the brim, while lakes and streams overflowed their banks.

Floods are dangerous, often have disastrous consequences, and need to be taken seriously. But what caught my attention was the requirement that the ground be saturated before the runoff could occur.

Just like flooding water, spiritual saturation must happen before the runoff can occur. If we want to overflow into the lives of others, we need to absorb all we can of God's mercy, love, grace, joy, and forgiveness. We cannot give away what we don't possess.

Paul writes to the Romans, *"May the God of hope fill you with all joy and peace as you trust in him, so that you may overflow with hope by the power of the Holy Spirit*" (Romans 15:13). God is eager to share His love, joy, peace, wisdom, and grace. Absorb all you can, and let His blessing overflow to those around you.

DAY 23
JUNK FOOD

The last day of a week-long backpacking trip in the Oregon Cascade Mountains, my brother and I were down to leftovers. So, we enjoyed a breakfast of freeze-dried blueberry dessert and a few crumbled chocolate chip cookies. Then lunch consisted of raisins, beef jerky, and peanuts. Not a bad start to the day.

As we took off our packs at the end of the hike, my brother Paul reminded me that we had not seen a vegetable for several days, and we should probably eat a *real meal.* I agreed so we stopped and had milkshakes for dinner.

Hey, it was vacation!

We can only subsist on junk food for so long and then—if we want to remain strong and healthy—we need real food. A tasty blueberry dessert for breakfast, fistfuls of peanuts for lunch, and a creamy milkshake for dinner are okay from time to time, but we need a regular diet of healthy basics if we want to enjoy good health.

Peter tells us, *"Like newborn babies, crave pure spiritual milk, so that by it you may grow up in your salvation"* (1 Peter 2:2a).

The writer of Hebrews takes this thought farther saying, "*But solid food is for the mature, who by constant use have trained themselves to distinguish good from evil*" (Hebrews 5:14).

Don't be a junk-food Christian. Make sure you eat a healthy portion of solid food every day. Read God's Word, chew on it, and let it provide the strength you need to serve God and walk with Him.

DAY 24
JOY AND STRENGTH

For many years, my wife, Cay, worked at our church running the preschool ministry. One Saturday afternoon, I was helping her prepare the classrooms for Sunday morning services. I was growing a little tired of moving chairs, vacuuming carpet, and putting colored pictures of Jonah on the classroom walls. I didn't have a really bad attitude, but I was ready to go home and relax.

Suddenly, Cay bounced enthusiastically into the room and said, "I really love my job."

I was working out of duty and love for my wife, but I was experiencing a personal energy crisis. I was missing the joy that recharged her batteries and sustained her efforts. Nehemiah said, "*The joy of the Lord is my strength*" (Nehemiah 8:10).

Are you working out of duty? Are you running low on energy? Is your strength giving out? Maybe gritting your teeth and doubling your effort is not the answer. Maybe falling in love with Jesus is what we need. The joy of the Lord provides strength when we are running on empty. His joy rejuvenates and sustains us for the long haul.

We all need breaks and we all need rest—that's the way God made us. But if your normal work patterns are draining your reserves, don't look to another cup of coffee to perk you up. Recapture the joy of the Lord and the strength He provides.

DAY 25
KEEP YOURSELVES
FROM IDOLS

We all worship something. We are natural worshippers because that is how we were designed. We were intended to worship God and Him alone. The problem is that many of us have misplaced the true object of our adoration and replaced it with an unworthy substitute.

The children of Israel lost contact with God while He and Moses chatted on Mount Sinai. They didn't stop worshipping; they just redirected their affections. They fashioned an alternative object—a golden calf—to absorb their expressions of adoration.

John has a seemingly innocuous statement at the end of his first epistle. He concludes First John with the command, *"Dear children, keep yourselves from idols"* (1 John 5:21). These six words seem like a mother reminding her children to "be good" as they walk out the door for school. But this command is much more than that; it is central to our lives and faith.

Some of us worship money; others popularity, education, positions of power, cars, fishing, cooking, performance, health, beauty, or a host of other things that can supplant God as the object of our adoration. None of them are worthy.

When something else—even a very good thing—has captured our attention, the real issue is our view of God. Once we catch a glimpse of His greatness and goodness, our only possible response is to make Him the object of our worship and the center of our lives.

The best way to keep ourselves from idols is to know and respond to the One we were designed to adore. Take time to reflect on who God is and what he has done. Share your thoughts with others, and worship Him alone.

DAY 26
REASONS FOR LOOKING BACK

Studies show that we generally attribute our success to hard work or intelligence. When things don't go well, we blame bad luck or others for our failures. Human nature takes the credit and shifts the blame.

Five times in the book of Deuteronomy we read the phrase: *"Remember that you were slaves in Egypt"* (5:15, 15:15, 16:12, 24:18, and 24:22). The reason for looking back and remembering is to maintain perspective in the present.

The command to remember is always coupled with directions for today. The retrospective on their years in slavery was to help the Israelites make wise and gracious decisions along life's journey. The five commands to look back correlated to five directives for godly living:

(1) Trusting God enough to rest one day a week
(2) Freeing others from slavery
(3) Giving generously to the work of the Lord
(4) Providing justice to the weak and vulnerable
(5) Caring for the needs of the poor

When we forget where we came from, we will begin to think we have earned our positions or possessions, and we deserve any blessing we may enjoy. Only when we remember that we, too, were once *slaves in Egypt* will we engage life with gratitude and humility.

DAY 27
HOLD ON

Life is painful. My prayer list seems to be growing longer every day. Cancer, heart attacks, strokes, accidents, loss of loved ones, bankruptcy, divorce, unemployment, relational tension. The list could go on and on.

I've encountered statistics (they seem accurate, but I've never been able to verify them) indicating that those who go through painful life circumstances often compound their problems by indulging in short-term, destructive fixes. Lose a child ... have an affair; diagnosed with cancer ... go on a spending binge; file for bankruptcy ... indulge in alcohol.

What really impresses me is when I observe friends overcoming life's most difficult challenges with grace and hope. I'm inspired and energized when I see people facing painful traumas clinging to God—and to each other—rather than looking for a quick-fix distraction.

Job faced his share of pain—losing his fortune, the death of his ten children, the distain of his wife, and criticism from his friends. Yet he found a way to hold on to his integrity and his relationship with God.

Even though Job's friends missed the mark with much of their advice, Elihu made a suggestion that is worth repeating thousands of years later:

Beware of turning to evil, which you seem to prefer to affliction (Job 36:21).

DAY 28
TIME STANDS STILL

The clocks in my office no longer tick. For years, the wall behind my desk held thirteen ticking clocks to remind me of the time in each of our CCI associations. But alas, no more.

The clocks are still there, but they are silent. As the batteries grew old, I decided not to replace them. Without the electricity, the clocks' hands remain motionless. They still look good. They still decorate my wall. But they don't do what they were designed to do—they don't tell time.

Without a power source, we will soon run out of energy and fail to fulfill our design. We can look good, but be very unproductive.

In an age before batteries, Jesus used the analogy of a vine and its branches to express the same idea. Jesus told his disciples:

> *I am the vine; you are the branches. If a man remains in me and I in him, he will bear much fruit; apart from me you can do nothing*
> (John 15:5).

Stay close to God. Don't let your spiritual battery run out of power. Rely on His strength to sustain you and to keep you fulfilling your God-given design.

DAY 29
ALL THINGS NEW

The owners desperately wanted to save the old building, but it was in terrible shape—leaky roof, dangerous asbestos, clogged plumbing, sagging foundation, and questionable electrical wiring.

After investing too much time and money, the owners finally capitulated and decided to tear down the dilapidated structure and start anew. Repairs could not fix the problem; a new structure was required.

Like the building owners, we all desire to fix our lives and renovate our dilapidated souls. But God does not want to patch our lives—He wants to make all things new.

Paul reminds us, "*Therefore, if anyone is in Christ, he is a new creation; the old has gone, the new has come!*" (2 Corinthians 5:17).

We desperately try to maintain the familiar brokenness of our past by putting a fresh coat of paint on a helpless and hopeless cause. But God desires to make us into something wonderful and new. That requires both a complete teardown and a total rebuild into something new that brings honor to the Builder and effectiveness to the structure.

DAY 30
TRAVELING LIGHT

The airlines haven't lost my luggage too often, but with enough frequency to make me carry-on everything I need whenever possible. Traveling light is an art that I'm still learning, but I always seem to have enough to wear and more "stuff" than I need. I rarely wish I had more with me, and usually get tired toting so much baggage through airports.

Traveling light is important on airplanes, but it is imperative in our spiritual life. We tend to collect unimportant baggage and accumulate destructive behaviors and attitudes as we move through life. We need to get rid of the things that slow us down or hold us back.

The writer of Hebrews tells us, *"Let us throw off everything that hinders and the sin that so easily entangles"* (Hebrews 12:1b). Getting rid of non-essentials is critical to our spiritual progress. Materialism, pride, lust, greed, and bitterness are just a few of the sins that can weigh us down and hold us back from getting where we need to go.

How do we get rid of the baggage? Hebrews 12 goes on to say, *"Let us fix our eyes on Jesus, the author and perfecter of our faith"* (Hebrews 12:2a). The more that we focus on Christ, the less important are the distractions and the less attractive the sin.

As we travel, let's go light. And let's stay focused on Jesus, who is all we truly ever need.

DAY 31
HAPPILY EVER AFTER

"And they lived happily ever after ... " is the familiar refrain that concludes most northern European fairy tales. After all the danger and challenge, fear and victory, the good guys move on to a happy life that never ends.

People only live "happily ever after" in folklore and make-believe. Or do they?

I wonder if the attraction of the happily-ever-after endings is because God designed us to experience them, to enjoy life with Him forever and ever? Maybe we love the simple hope of a happy, peaceful, and fulfilled ever-after because it resonates with God's offer to each of us.

The hope of Christianity includes a transformed and abundant life now, but also encompasses spending eternity with God—the ultimate "happily ever after."

The apostle John recorded the words of Jesus:

For my Father's will is that everyone who looks to the Son and believes in him shall have eternal life, and I will raise him up at the last day (John 6:40).

Later John said it this way:

I write these things to you who believe in the name of the Son of God so that you may know that you have eternal life (1 John 5:13).

Fairy tales have some rough and dangerous moments, but the end is always secure. Follow Christ through the difficulties of today. Live life to the fullest. And look forward to the blessed hope of a *happily ever after* ....

ABOUT THE AUTHOR

Dan Bolin is the International Director of Christian Camping International-Worldwide. Dan has been involved in Christian camping for fifty years. He and his wife Cay served at Pine Cove Christian Camps in Tyler, Texas for twenty-five years. They have been married for thirty-nine years, and have one daughter who lives with her husband in Washington, DC. Dan is the author of seven books and speaks throughout the United States and around the world.

CPSIA information can be obtained
at www.ICGtesting.com
Printed in the USA
FSOW04n2342150316
17960FS